The Manner and Solemnitie of the Coronation of
... Charles the Second, at Manchester, 1661, by
W. Heawood. Also, the Celebration of the
Coronation of ... King George Iii. and Queen
Charlotte, at Manchester, 1761 Extr. from
Harrop's Manchester Mercury. Followed by an
Account of the Procession of the Different
Trades, by T. Barritt. With Biogr. Notices of the
Principal Persons Taking Part in Each
Celebration
by William Heawood

Address:
HardPress
8345 NW 66TH ST #2561

G. H. Lewes.

THE

MANNER AND SOLEMNITIE

OF

THE CORONATION

OF

HIS MOST GRACIOUS MAJESTIE

KING CHARLES THE SECOND,

AT MANCHESTER,

IN THE COUNTIE PALATINE OF LANCASTER,

On the 23rd day of April, 1661.

By *WILLIAM HEAWOOD, Gentleman.*

ALSO

THE CELEBRATION OF THE CORONATION

OF THEIR

MOST GRACIOUS MAJESTIES

King George III. and Queen Charlotte,

AT MANCHESTER,

On the 22nd day of September, 1761.

WITH

BIOGRAPHICAL NOTICES OF THE PRINCIPAL PERSONS
TAKING PART IN EACH CELEBRATION.

LONDON:

JOHN CAMDEN HOTTIN, PICCADILLY.

1863.

Arch Bodl. A.

IV. 8.

Four copies on vellum.
49 copies on small and 23 copies on large paper.

———

Imprinted at Manchester, in the Countie Palatine of Lancaster,
By Alex. Ireland and Co., Pall Mall Court.
MDCCCLXII.

———

For Private Circulation only.

MANNER OF THE SOLEMNITIE

OF THE

KINGS CORONATION,

AT MANCHESTER, IN LANCASTER,

April 23, 1661.

WORTHY SIR,

Hitherto I perceive the actings of your friends in this place, upon the day of his Majesties Coronation, hath not bin communicated by any pen to a publick view, and least that silence might eclipse their loyall observing of that day, or you otherwise perswaded of it, be pleased to accept of this accompt from a rude hand. On Monday the 22 of April, being the day before his Majesties Coronation, that worthy and valiant Gentleman Maj. John Byrom,(¹)

(¹) John Byrom, of Salford, Esq., aged 44 years, in 1664, Sergeant-Major in the regiment of Lancashire Militia, commanded by Col. Roger Nowell, on the part of King Charles.

In 1646 he compounded with the Commissioners of Sequestration for his estates for £201. 16s. 6d., whilst his brother, Edmund Byrom, of Salford, com-

b

(whose fidelitie hath bin sufficiently testified by his great sufferings for his constancy in his Majesties service) did command his Foot Companie being Freeholders, and consisting of an huńdred and fourtié men, well arm'd and disciplin'd, to attend the Solemnization of the day ; who all being in readiness, the next morning drew forth into the Field ; whither likewise Nicholas Mosley, Esq.,(¹) a sufferer for his

pounded for £2. 6s. 8d., and his uncle, Sir Thomas Prestwich, Bart., and Thomas Prestwich, Esq., his son, were required to pay into the same treasury £330.

Mr. Heywood (Newcome's Diary Chet. Soc. Publications, p. 42, note) says the Cavalier, John Byrom, was Major of the Manchester Trainbands, and the leader of the town's rejoicings at the Restoration.

This gallant royalist officer, who had been through life consistent in the maintenance of his political and religious opinions was, after the Restoration, in the commission of the peace for the county of Lancaster. He was buried in the Derby Chapel, within the Collegiate Church of Manchester, March 11th, 1667-8, in the 59th year of his age. He married Mary, daughter and co-heiress of William Radcliffe, of Foxdenton, Esq.

(¹) " Nicholas Mosley was the eldest son of Oswald Mosley, Esq., of Ancoats. He was baptized at the Collegiate Church, Manchester, in 1611, and was a minor at his father's death. Upon the breaking out of the Civil War, he adhered to the cause of the unfortunate Charles, and was subjected on that account to the severe displeasure of the Parliament, together with his uncle Francis, and his cousin Nicholas, of Collyhurst. Their estates were confiscated in 1643 ; but on August 16th, 1646, in the House of Commons, an order for granting a pardon to Nicholas Mosley, of the Ancoates, in the county of Lancaster, gentleman, was read and passed, and ordered to be sent up to the Lords, who confirmed this order. Upon his reverse of fortune, he turned his attention to literary pursuits, and in the year 1653 he published ' A Treatise on the Passions and Faculties of the Soul of Man,' in three books, the first of which he dedicated to his nephew, Robert Booth, Esq. ; the second to his brother, Edward Mosley, Esq. ; and the third to his much honoured friend and neighbour, Humphrey Chetham, Esq. ; to late Majestie, Captaine of the Auxilliaries raised in the Towne for the defence of his Majesties most Royal Person and Prerogative, did march into the same Field with his Companie, consisting of above two hundred and twentie men, most of them being of the better sort of this place, and bearing their own Armes, in great gallantrie and rich Scarffes, expressing themselves with manie great acclamations of joy and freeness to serve his Majestie. The Ensigne for the Auxilliaries was blew and white ; and in the middle a very rich Crown of Gold on both sides, with this mottoe under written, *Vincit qui Patitur:* carried by Mr. William Byrom([1]) of this Towne, and at whose

these was prefixed an Epistle Dedicatory to his honoured kinsman Robert Booth. Printed for Humphrey Mosley, at the Princes Arms, St. Paul's Churchyard, in 1653."

" When Charles II. was restored to the throne of these realms, he evinced the most sincere gratification ; and upon the coronation of that King (23 April, 1661), he mustered the remnant of an auxiliary band, which he had himself raised for the defence of his late Majesty, and which still consisted of 220 men of the better sort, with whom he proceeded through the streets of the town at the head of a splendid procession, attended by the Warden and Fellows of the Collegiate Church, the Boroughreeve and other town's officers, together with a numerous concourse of neighbouring gentry. After celebrating this joyful event in a series of festivities for the space of a whole week, this loyal band were dismissed with an appropriate address from their Captain." Memoirs of the Mosley family, by Sir O. Mosley, Bart. Privately printed.

([1]) William Byrom took an active part, during the seventeenth century, in promoting the cause of Parliament. On the 12th day of August, 1656, he was one of the burgesses and chief inhabitants of Manchester who elected Richard Radcliffe, of Pool Fold, Esq., as a burgess of that town, to represent them in the Commonwealth Parliament. In 1657 he was Boroughreeve of Manchester. He

charge the said Ensigne was wholly made.   In their
marching off the Field, and so to the Church, Major
Byrom's Companie had the Van; and before Captain
Mosley's Companie, marched in honour of the day
fourtie young Boyes, about the age of seven years, all
cloathed in white Stuffe, Plumes of Feathers in their
Hatts, blew Scarffes, armed with little Swords hanging
in black Belts, and short Pikes shouldered; and in the
Rear of the said Captain's Companie, another Companie of elder Boyes about twelve yeares of age, with
Musquets and Pikes, Drums beating, and Colours
flieing marched in order; all which being decentlie
drawn up in the Churchyard, laid down their Armes,
and so passed into the Church to hear the Sermon
prepared for that day, at which time there was such a
concourse of people, who civilly and soberly demeaned
themselves all the whole day, the like never seen in
this, nor the like place.   The Reverend Richard Hey-
ricke(¹) Warden of this College, made an Orthodox

was the friend and patron of Newcome, and was Newcome's landlord in 1660.
He was married at the Collegiate Church, April 7th, 1640, to Rebecca, daughter
of Captain John Beswicke, of Manchester, and was buried at the same place,
December 24th, 1666, ætat. 48.   At the Restoration he took a part in the
rejoicings, being Ensign in the Auxilliaries.

(¹) Richard Heyrick, B.D., Warden, was educated at Oxford.   He was
appointed to the Wardenship in 1636, obtained for him in reversion by his father
(Sir William Heyrick, of Beaumanor Park, Leicestershire), in lieu of a debt
owing to his family by the crown.   He died August 6th, 1667, and was buried
near the altar of the Collegiate Church, over which he had presided during the
greater part of one of the most turbulent periods of England's history.

Sermon upon these words, 2 *Kings, Chap. xi. verse* 12. *Then he brought out the Kings Son, and put the Crown upon him, and gave him the testimony, and they made him King, and anointed him, and they clapt their hands, and said, God save the KING,* which Sermon is now in Press. (¹)   After Sermon from the Church marched in their order the Burroughreeve, Constables, and the rest of the Burgesses of this Towne not then in Armes, accompanied with Sir Ralph Ashton, Knight and Baronet, (²) and divers neighbouring Gentlemen of qualitie, together with the said Warden, Fellows of the said Colledg, and divers other Ministers, with the Town-Musick playing before them upon loud Instruments through the Streets to the Cross, (³) and so for-

(¹) A Sermon preached at the Collegiate Church, Manchester, on Tuesday the 23rd of April, 1661, being the Coronation day of his Royal Majesty Charles II., by Richard Heyrick, Warden of the said Colledge.   Lond : Printed for Ralph Shelmerdine, Bookseller in Manchester, 1661.
So remarkably rare is this Sermon, that, when the late Dr. Hibbert Ware was writing the " History of the Foundations of Manchester," the publishers of that work advertised all over the country for it, but were unsuccessful in procuring a copy ; the only one then known was in the British Museum, a transcript of which is printed entire in the first volume of the above work.

(²) Sir Ralph Ashton, Bart., was born in 1626, knighted by Charles I. ; M.P. for Clithero, and created a baronet 12th of Charles II. ; died 23rd of April, 1665. He was the son of Ralph Ashton, Esq., M.P., a colonel in the Royalist army ; he represented Clithero in the time of Charles I., and the county in the 16th of Charles I. ; died 17th of February, 1652.   His son took a prominent part in the rejoicings at Manchester at the Restoration.

(³) The ancient Market Cross, Stocks, and Pillory, stood in the Market Place, opposite the end of the present Fish Market, and were removed in 1816.

c

wards to the Conduit, Officers and Souldiers in their orders ; the Gentlemen and Officers drunck his Majesties health in Claret running forth at three streames of the said Conduit,(¹) which was answered from the Souldiery by a great volley of shot, and many great shouts, saying, *God save the King:* which being ended, the Gentry and Ministers went to Dinner, attended with the Officers and Musick of the Towne ; the Auxilliaries dineing at the same place ; during the time of dinner, and until after Sun-set, the said Conduit did run with pure Claret, which was freely drunke by all that could, for the croud, come near the same ; after an houre, or something more spent in dinner, the drums did beat, and the Souldiers marched into the Field again, giving three great vollies and shouts, making the Country therewith to Eccho ; and from thence through several streets, bringing the said Major Byrom to his own house, where making an halt, the Major began his Majesties health in Sack to the Officers, the Souldiers standing in Rankes and

(¹) The Conduit, which stood on the westerly side of the old Exchange, and nearly on the site now occupied by the large gas lamp, opposite to the entrance into St. Ann's Square, was erected in 1506, at the sole expense of Elizabeth Beck, widow and sole heir of Richard Bexwicke, an eminent merchant of that period, and a public benefactor of the town ; the Conduit was supplied from a spring at the top of King-street (from whence the present Spring Gardens derives its name) ; in 1776 the spring was by some means destroyed, and the Conduit becoming useless was most likely then taken down.

This is the earliest recorded instance of an attempt to supply the inhabitants of Manchester with water.

Files likewise drank the same, and Ecchoed it forth with several vollies and acclamations of joy : so from the Major's house marched round about Salford, fireing and shouting all along ; and again at the door of the Major's Ensign's house another halt was made, and the Companies were drawne round in Single File in the street, there freely entertained with Sack and Claret, returning of thanks with vollies of shot and great shouts ; marched back into this Towne, and after some few vollies and shouts ; were taken up with raine ; Bonefires being in every street, and thereby prevented from marching ; the Bells continued ringing night and day ; some fire-works runing upon cords the length of one hundred yards, and so backwards, with crackers in the ayre, which sport continued till almost midnight, but spectators much disappointed by the raine, all the day being very clear and glorious, Bone-fires burning above a week.

Unto which suffer me to adde these ensuing lines : That after Captain Mosley had received intelligence of the joyful, glorious, and prosperous carrying on of the day at London, without prejudice in that great con-course, being honored with the brightness of the Sun, unto which day the heavens gave testimony of their assent, did upon the 1 of May march his Com-panie into the Field, and there in the middle of them, being drawne round, made a learned Speech, declaring

the goodness of God to this Nation in the happy resto-
ring of his Majestie to his just Right and Priviledg,
beyond all the expectation of man, useing arguments of
obedience, and grounds of thanks for his Majesties
preservation, and praying *for his Majesties long and*
happy Reign over these Nations, all the people cryed
God save the King, his Speech was long, only I say
he made a Speech ; this ended, the Companie as
before with the young Boyes marched into the Towne,
and were civilly entertained by Dr. Howarth,([1]) and
others of their march, and being drawn up at the
Cross and thereabout, all bare-headed drunck his
Majesties health in Sack and Claret, at the charge of
Mr. Halliwel,([2]) giving a volley and shout, marched
through several streets, still fireing and rejoycing until

([1]) Theophilus Howarth, M.D., of Howarth Hall, was baptized at Rochdale,
2nd of January, 1613-14 ; entered of Magdalen College, Cambridge, M.D., July
2nd, 1661 ; married Mary, daughter of Henry Ashurst, of Ashurst, in the county
of Sussex, Esq. ; and was a resident in Manchester, where he was an able and
active magistrate, and much esteemed by the Royalist party. He died on the 9th
of April, 1671, at Manchester, where he had distinguished himself by his fidelity
to the cause of Charles I., and was buried on the 12th of the same month, within
the vaults of the Collegiate Church. He was an attesting witness to the will of
Humphrey Chetham, December 8th, 1651, and had doubtless attended that good
and charitable man in his last illness.

([2]) James Halliwel appears to have been related to the Byroms, having married
Ann Byrom, widow of Mr. John Bibby, of Manchester, October 18th, 1664. He
was buried at the Collegiate Church, April 15th, 1665. This Mr. Halliwel is
often mentioned by Newcome in his diary, and also in his Autobiography. (See
Chetham Soc. Publications.)

evening, then lodg'd their Colours, discharging the Companie until the 29th of May instant, being his Majesties birth-day, and the day of his glorious return to Whitehall, which is intended here with thankfulness, and all manner of rejoycing to be observed. It is desired that this should be printed, and though it come later, yet it is not inferior to many greater places. I could not give a true Narrative in fewer lines, and therefore be pleased to excuse the prolixity, and great trouble you are put unto, occasioned by your reall Friends, and subscribed by

Your Affectionate Kinsman and Servant,

WILLIAM HEAWOOD.

Manchester, May 7, 1661.

d

CELEBRATION

OF

THE CORONATION

OF

King George III. and Queen Charlotte,

AT MANCHESTER,

September 22nd, 1761.

THE following extract, from the only newspaper then
published in Manchester (" Harrop's Manchester
Mercury "), is all the notice taken of the Procession and Rejoicings which took place in this town,
at the Coronation of King George III. and his
Queen ; the Programme of the Procession of Trades
has been transcribed from a MS. of the late Mr.
Thomas Barritt, in the Chetham Library, who was
curious in preserving anything of the sort, and was
most likely an eye witness ; it was therefore con-
sidered by the Editor a fitting accompaniment to the

account of the proceedings, just 100 years prior, at the Coronation of Charles II. :—

[September 29th, 1761.]—" Last Tuesday (Sept. 22nd) being the day appointed for the Coronation of their Majesties (George III. and Queen Charlotte), the same was ushered in with firing of cannon and ringing of bells, and about eleven o'clock in the morning, the workmen in the several branches of trade being formed into companies, with their proper emblems and devices, went in procession through the town, amidst the greatest concourse of people ever assembled here.

" About three in the afternoon, all the principal inhabitants, with favors in their hats, in honour of the day, attended on horseback upon the Boroughreeve(¹) and Constables, and with them paraded through the Square and principal streets of the town. Several

(¹) Edward Byrom, of Byrom, Kersall Cell, and Manchester, Esq., son and heir, and nephew, heir-at-law, and devisee in fee of his uncle, Edward Byrom, Esq. ; born 13th of June, 1724, and baptised 24th of June, 1724, at the Collegiate Church, Manchester ; married March, 1750, to Eleanora, daughter of William Halsted, of Lymm, county of Chester, Esq. He died April 21st, 1773, and was buried in the Byrom Chapel, Collegiate Church.

He served the office of Boroughreeve, 1761 [Constables, Henry Fielding and John Tipping], and also founded and endowed St. John's Church, in Manchester, the first stone of which was laid by himself, April 28th, 1768, consecrated June 7th, 1769, being the first of two munificent gifts from the same family towards the spiritual welfare of the inhabitants of Manchester. The second gift is the Church of the Holy Trinity, in Stretford New Road, built and endowed at the sole expense of Miss E. Atherton, granddaughter of the above ; the first stone was laid December 2nd, 1841 ; consecrated June 28th, 1843.

oxen and sheep were roasted whole, in different parts of the town and Salford. Three stages were erected, one in St. Ann's Square, one at the Cross, and one in Within Grove, from which a number of barrels of beer and wine were distributed amongst the populace.

" An entertainment was provided at the Old Coffee House,(¹) and another at the Bull's Head Inn,(²) for

(¹) The "Old Coffee House" formerly stood on the site of the present Exchange Street, the entrance to it being up a passage then called the "Dark Entry," a narrow footway, leading from the Market Place to St. Ann's Square. These buildings were pulled down 1777, to form the present Exchange Street.

(²) The Bull's Head Inn in the Market Place, at that time the principal one in the town, has now no higher pretensions than that of a first class public-house. It must then have been considerably larger than it is now, or otherwise the accommodation could hardly have been sufficient for all the great folk it was in the habit of receiving; even royalty itself has not hesitated to seek a shelter under its hospitable roof, and that more than once. Shorn as it is of its former grandeur, if we may judge from the portly dimensions of its present worthy hostess, as many of the good things of this life are still to be had there, and of as high a quality, as at any of the more princely though juvenile establishments in the town. It is one of the few remaining specimens of the snug and quiet retreats selected by our forefathers to enjoy their afternoon's glass and pipe of fragrant weed in, after the business of the day was over; and, if bricks could speak, how many goodly "quiffs and cranks," and stories of hair-breadth escapes by "flood and field," related by the jolly old race of "Bump the Bags" [a slang term for commercial travellers of the *olden time*, who used to *locomote* on horseback, with their patterns inclosed in a pair of *saddle-bags*], should we be made familiar with! In 1610 Richard Halliwell was the landlord of the Bull's Head, and appears to have been a person of good reputation in his day as a vintner. He supplied the churchwardens of Rochdale, Middleton, and other neighbouring parishes for a series of years with wine for the communion; and on several occasions, when marriage licenses were applied for at the Court of Chester, "Mr. Halliwell, of the Bull," gave "satisfaction" that the parties were of age, and had proper legal consent. In 1627 he served the office of Boroughreeve. In 1629 "Mr. Richard Halliwell, of Manchester, and Mrs. Margaret Lockyer" were married at Rochdale; but no wife is mentioned in his will, dated 12th of May,

e

the repast of the gentlemen, from whence they adjourned to the Exchange to conclude the evening, by drinking the healths of their most gracious Sovereign and the Queen.

" The whole town was most splendidly illuminated ; and notwithstanding so many thousand people were assembled, there was not the least disorder or tumult, an undeniable proof of their affection for the best of Kings.

" On the Wednesday following, in the evening, there was a Ball in the Exchange,(¹) at which were

1638, wherein he styles himself " Richard Halliwell, of Manchester, senr., vintner, and desires that his body may be buryed within the Parish Church of Manchester." He devises to his eldest son, Richard Halliwell, a good landed estate, and names his sons James and Samuel, and several daughters and sons-in-law, and requests his " friend the Right Worshipful Roger Downes, Esq.," to be his overseer. The effects were sworn before Edmund Hopwood, of Hopwood, Esq., March 29th, 1639, and the will was proved at Chester. Which of the above sons succeeded to their father's business is not known.

(¹) The Old Exchange formerly stood between the Market Place and the present Victoria Street, on the ground once better known as " Penni-less Hill," and opposite to the present Exchange. It was erected in 1729 by Sir Oswald Mosley, the then lord of the manor : the ground floor was used as a Market-House, and the room above as the Exchange. It was taken down in 1792, and on the spot was erected a stone obelisk, which went by the name of " Nathan Crompton's Folly," he being Boroughreeve at the time of its erection ; in 1816 this was removed, and was placed in the garden (where it now is) of the late Mr. William Yates, at the house erected by him out of the old black and white timber houses taken down in Market Street when that street was widened in 1822. This house stands on the right hand as you enter upon Stony Knolls ; it was then, and probably is now, better known by some as " Yates' Whim !" having cost him more to carry out his " whim " than would have sufficed to build a brick mansion of four times its size. This gentleman eventually emigrated to South Australia, where he died, if not in great poverty, certainly in very reduced circumstances ; he married a daughter of the late Joseph Harrop, proprietor of the " Manchester Mercury."

present near seven hundred ladies and gentlemen, and in an apartment contiguous a very grand collation of fruits, sweetmeats, and confectionary of all sorts, was disposed in a very elegant manner."—*Harrop's Manchester Mercury, Tuesday, Sept.* 29, 1761.

AN ACCOUNT

OF THE

PROCESSION OF THE DIFFERENT TRADES,

WHO WALKED AT MANCHESTER,

September 22, 1761,

BEING THE

CORONATION DAY

OF

King George III. and Queen Charlotte.

The Procession of the Tailors.

A Person in a proper livery to clear the way.
Six Pikemen, two and two.
Adam and Eve, in cloaths made of green ivy leaves, with apple tree and serpent.
A Banner, with the Arms of the County displayed.

The Champion, representing Sir John Hawksworth,
with his Aid de Camp, on horseback.
Sixteen Men dress'd in scarlet, with light blue sashes
and laced hats, with truncheons.
A grand band of musick.
The Coat of Arms of the Trade displayed.
· Fourteen Pikemen, two and two.   Lastly,
The rest of the trade, genteelly dress'd in coloured
cloaths.

The Procession of the Woolcombers.

Two Stewards, with white wands.
A band of musick.
Arms of Bishop Blaize.
The Treasurer and Secretary.
A Page Royal, with white wand.
Bishop Blaize on horseback, attended by ten pages
on foot.
The Members, two and two, with wool wiggs, sashes,
and cockades of the same.
Two Junior Stewards, with each a white wand and
other decorations.

The Procession of the Worsted Weavers.

A Shepherd and Shepherdess, attended by three
boys and three girls, as pages, under a triumphal arch

of laurel, in the centre of which is placed
a golden fleece.
Twenty-four Apprentices, in holland shirts and white
caps, with white wands.
A Captain of Grenadiers on horseback.
Four Grenadiers, two and two.
An Ensign, bearing the Weavers' Arms.
Two drums and two fifes.
Sixteen Grenadiers, two and two. On the front of the
Grenadiers' caps is woven the weavers' arms,
in which is also their mottoe,
"*In God is our Hope*," and on some of their belts is
wove, "God bless King George III. and
Queen Charlotte," and on others, " The bells shall ring
for George our King."
The Champion in armour, on horseback.
A band of musick.
An Imperial Crown, borne on a velvet cushion.
The King and Queen in a chariot, drawn by six horses,
with three postillions in scarlet, with black
caps trimm'd with gold. Over the heads of the King
and Queen is borne the Royal Arms ;
on the right hand the Archbishop of Canterbury ;
on the left the Archbishop of York, both on horseback,
with proper pages attending.
A Captain of Hussars.
Twelve Hussars, two and two.

f

A considerable number of Pikemen, two and two.
Two Men, one clothed with figured gartering, the other
with diaper work, with caps of the same.
The Representatives of the Trade, with truncheons
tipp'd with gold, with sashes and cockades
of their own weaving.
A Carriage, on which is a person at work on a single
loom, representing the original of the trade.
A considerable number of Pikemen, two and two.
An Old Woman spinning time.
A Banner displayed, on which is this mottoe, " God
bless the King and Queen, and success to trade."

The Procession of the Shoemakers.

Two Pioneers.
Robin Hood in scarlet, and his Men in green, with
bows and quivers of arrows.
Twelve Grenadiers with a standard.
Page.——Crispianus and his Aid de Camp on
horseback.——Page.
The Crown and Cushion on horseback, supported by
two Yeomen of the Guard, two Pages to lead
the horse, and two others following.
Crispin and Ozella on horseback, with four Pages
supporting Ozella's train.
Drums and fifes.

Twelve Body Guards,
The Captain of the Apprentices.
The Body of Apprentices.
The brave Colonel Salter.
The Journeymen.
The Sword Bearer and two maces.
Band of musick.
Sir Simon Eyre, Lord Mayor of London.
Two Aldermen in scarlet cloaks.
Closed with the Masters and Wardens of the Companie,
with green staffes and gold heads.

The Procession of the Dyers.

Twelve aged Men of the trade, two and two.
The Warden on horseback, bearing the Arms of the
Companie, attended by eight Pages on foot,
with white wands.
About forty Persons of the trade, in holland shirts,
with sashes of various colours, black breeches,
and white stockings.

The Procession of the Joiners.

The Sword Bearer.
The Clerk, with a white wand, tipp'd with green
and blue.
The Banner Bearer, with the Arms of the Trade
display'd.

Two Stewards, with white wands, tipp'd with
green and blue.
The remainder of the Trade in green aprons, white
gloves, and cockades, two and two.

The Procession of the Silk Weavers.[1]

The Chairman, with blue and red sashes, crossed.
Four Stewards, with pink sashes and blue wands,
tipp'd with gold.
Twelve Men, with blue scarffes and blue truncheons,
tipp'd with gold, two and two.
The Banner of the Trade.

[1] " When *Georgius Secundus* ascended to heaven
" And the Crown of these Realms to his Grandson was given
" The folks of Mancunium made needful oblation
" By splendidly keeping the King's Coronation,
" Tho' the Whigs laugh'd and said, it was ' labour in vain
" To endeavour to wash out the Jacobite stain.'
" The procession of Trades, proved how much Trade had got on,
" But amidst all the workmen—no weavers of Cotton ! "

Aston's Metrical Records of Manchester.

[Silk weavers and worsted weavers were in the procession in honour of the
coronation of George III., but no cotton weavers, the few then employed in that branch perhaps walking with the weavers of the more
common fabricks.]—*Note to Met. Records.*

The late Dr. Percival computed the number of inhabitants of Manchester and
Salford, in 1757, at 19,839, and in 1774, of Manchester alone, at 22,481 ; what
it might be in 1761 there is now no means of ascertaining, but we may naturally
conclude that in 1861, just 100 years after, the number employed in cotton spinning and weaving alone is more than the entire population of the town was at
the former period.

Band of musick.
The remainder of the Trade, two and two, in their proper dresses.
The Clerk, to bring up the rear, with two green sashes, crossed, two silver pens on his breast, carrying a wand tipp'd with gold.

The Procession of Hatters.

Two Persons of the Trade with gigantick hats on.
The Standard Bearer, in a fur coat, with the Arms of the Trade.
Two Persons on horseback, dressed in Russian fur skins, and caps of fur, two Pages to attend, each dressed in white, with fur caps and sashes.
Four Persons with red hats.
Four Persons with green hats.
Four Persons with dark blue hats.
Four Persons with Saxon green hats.
Four Persons with Saxon blue hats.
And a number of the Trade with white hats, two and two, brought up the rear of the procession.

FINIS.

Im The Story
personalised classic books

"Beautiful gift.. lovely finish.
My Niece loves it, so precious!"

Helen R Brumfieldon

UNIQUE GIFT

FOR KIDS, PARTNERS
AND FRIENDS

Timeless books such as:

Kids

Alice in Wonderland · The Jungle Book · The Wonderful Wizard of Oz
Peter and Wendy · Robin Hood · The Prince and The Pauper
The Railway Children · Treasure Island · A Christmas Carol

Adults

Romeo and Juliet · Dracula

Highly Customizable

Change Books Title

Replace Characters Names with yours

Upload Photo it's inside page)

Add Inscriptions

Visit
Im The Story .com
and order yours today!